Body Thesaurus

BODY THESAURUS

POEMS

JENNIFER MILITELLO

TUPELO PRESS
NORTH ADAMS, MASSACHUSETTS

Library of Congress Cataloging-in-Publication Data available
upon request.
Cover and text designed by Bill Kuch.
First edition: May 2013.

Tupelo Press
P.O. Box 1767
243 Union Street, Eclipse Mill, Loft 305
North Adams, Massachusetts 01247
Telephone: (413) 664–9611 / Fax: (413) 664–9711
editor@tupelopress.org / www.tupelopress.org

Tupelo Press is an award-winning independent literary press that publishes
fine fiction, nonfiction, and poetry in books that are a joy to hold as well as
read. Tupelo Press is a registered 501(c)3 nonprofit organization, and we rely
on public support to carry out our mission of publishing extraordinary work
that may be outside the realm of the large commercial publishers. Financial
donations are welcome and are tax deductible.

"Man was matter . . . "
　　　—Joseph Heller

"I, in my intricate image, stride on two levels ..."
　　　—Dylan Thomas

CONTENTS

⚘

The self is not what is said about the self.

The self is not a study of the world.

The self is not a cure.

✠

The Skins We Slit Seeking the Vertebrae of Snakes

Then the color blue, like the pupil music dilates
inside us, throws wet on the line a twisted dress,
so free of the body's stem that within its shape

a storm is seen. This, the leaves preening
themselves against a delicate wind. The small cells
beating together until there is a system.

Truth brings in its hissing room. The doorknobs
to consequence turned in our sleep.
To have the song *disorder* about my branches,

its wine-black aftertaste sweet razors in the mix,
when the obvious violins beginning leave us
lemmings at the cliffs: silence's synapses firing.

At the fringe of stillness, I move. Witness me:
I am outside. With a million irises like gasoline.
The machine in us becomes what mixes

to make a man, what picks him from a pile
of bones. Drink from this and it will itch
in you, bewitch you, cause you to begin.

An ankle twisting in my chest. Once it ignites,
how slowly it burns. Its cage hangs above the sea:
inside, the sky is a pinned corsage.

The self is not a shadow of the self.

Personality State: Prophet

I asked to be made in the image of the Lord,
as an ode to a god I'd forgotten.
I paled like a throat of birch.
I paled at the thought of such fast wings.

I preferred the god of beating to the god
of flightless limbs. I chipped bit by bit
at the bones of this until I had a voice to take me
by the hand. I preferred the god of fragments.

Each small animal fallen wild. What I thought
was cold cried in the night like an abandoned well.
Snow falling not far from here, the verb of
what will listen. The cold stretch of terrace

in the moon. Away where evening sings
its wet leaves clustered like flint, its font
an insomnia from which we crack, its retinas
as clock-beautiful as logic. I remembered the name

of the closeness of dark, its carriages rolling
back through time to yoke the ghosts of oxen.
I could see its cry already like a weapon at the anvil,
its stethoscope that cannot find the heart.

Personality State: Scavenger's Daughter

I want to look prim if not proper, twist modestly
if not sedate. I want to give fate a reason
to hate me and exhaust me and lick me up.
I want my taste on the lips. I want to give shivers
living like lovers, and prayers when I cannot.

I want to break the way the branch predicts.
Break the veins, a village. Break the outer outside
first. Break the wear to market. Break
the hand with work. Break the gesture. Break
its jerk. Break to know the goldrush want.

Multiply the world by its wreckage, and come out
ahead, hearing dawn as it barks from the holds
of ships, landing quick like music with its crack
of whips, from the holds of a game I cannot
watch. I want to sin at the eaves of heaven.

One eye to the nowhere periscope of sleep.
A stiff gene that fits, an x where I have been.
The many bicycles of memory and their many
broken chains. I want hours to happen,
beehive-rich, and leave the watchman lame.

I want my God with no religion. I want to want
the tangled larceny of thirst. I want my heart
to have such branches its Octobers dream.
Little brevity, little jealousy of larks. Flock
of road, wind forbidden, excellence of coast.

Personality State: Persephone

I have seen the silhouettes that bring me heavens,
I have seen my torso, in hours of torn,
ripple laden with captivity, rent with cries
and the sky's white sheet drying in the wind,
weeping, a splash of oceans gone by, reeds,
and rains reciting an archery of wounds.

The twinned nights. In one I cry, in one
I recite historic tales. In both I never sleep.
My hands have the skulls of hawks. They prey
on those small bodies; they are blind, eyeless,
stars show them the way. Their sockets
see four winds as the directions of the earth.
Men on horseback. Forests asleep with the drums
at their hearts. The sky tells of its hooks.

‡‡

Cast the spells that wend me shut. Sew cloaks
of cartilage for gathering courage. Bend the hand
where it moans in place. Pry open the jaws
of an average wolf and infest it with your breath.

Do not speak in riddles. Do not speak for days.
I have seen myself dead at the hands of the sea.
I have seen myself trembling beneath a streetlamp
while my waist cried out, while my eyes were black
as mandolins and dawn was the fall of breaking glass.

‡‡

Punishment: carnivorous, its sunflower's wilt.
The caged bird empties its image into wind,
its small heart a tambourine, its black tongue
a gypsy cymbal counting out the rain
into the gloom ripening at a gull's pupil.
My hands, pale as ferns underwater.

I know the hours' mummification by heart.
Some mornings, chaste as corners, leave behind
their murmurs like nostalgia or need, to ghost them
with my own mudless scatter. When the sea runs barren
as the possible bones, when the names are gone
from the gravestones and cliffs, when the long dry dune
can decay us at last, November: a rhythm of bells.
Images of distance burn to death. Weathervanes
lean. The wheat has a wind-violence in it yet.

Personality State: Animal

I am only wolves, a thin endless shiver of what
is undernourished, of what I once saw drinking
with its stone-cold tongue at the plethora of rain.

Whispers prowl the bloodhounds of my heart.
My past circles the highway like a bird of prey.
I stay beneath its lazy romance, its wingspan

as vast as my senses. Those who bloom go
sleepless. Those who are fed the Novocain earth.
My body an estranged fixture, bent impure.

All is wrong. If I remember the world at all,
it is as an eclipse, as shadow's lace, its tresses
made from the shepherds of dusk, as hours decomposing.

Far from the eye, my circumstances see.
Death: its mere parasol baptized me once.
My memories are necklaces made from its teeth.

Personality State: Convict

The moon is a sudden pilgrim in a wheatless grove,
fermenting black in the rambling sigh,
in summer's fade, in a thrill of soon and violets.

Shapes of cold are made inside me, blind as mice
at birth. So few dead at the bottom of the river,
so few rapids broken open with their backs.

I empty bottles at the lips of the burn.
Four dramatic winds press into my hip to uproot
an infidel's heaven. I do not remember

how to sing. I tie together loosely certain papers
of my rage. I tie in little ribbons little packages
of light. In the night, there is a September.

Personality State: Statue

Winds start. The black forest fills soft
with all its particles hanging.

Braids my wrecked, unruly hair.
Invents a form of prayer
that does not fold its hands.

Wet leaves cling. A winter journeys
through the tendons to my wrist.
I remain until the surface stills
or gravity gentles like a lion at the hand.

Alcoves change. Cold dawns its tendrils.
The world has its cabins of shadow outstretched.
Its leafless birds, its shapeless animals,
its derelict hearts tepid and uncapped.

The world has its stone eye staggering to see,
has its hearts of spoiled singing.

My fingertips like windless landscapes
blur, pale as letters I'll never read;
meanwhile, their oblivions seek
to harness an insomnia of horses.

Personality State: Husk

When I say herons, but mean not so thin.

When the handkerchief is dropped, the race
started, the duel declared, the handgun shot.

The net that gathers nightingales
and weeps them toward the sky.

The stake to which time's blind pony
is tethered.

Rough mortar mixed with the blood of an ox.
Starless parchment of the roar-deep earth.

A hollow bottled like the sea.

The self is not a symptom.

Felon's Logic

Dear body I do not resent,
experiment with me.

I feel my mind grow broad as orchestras,
I feel its oceans weep. How I fall

awake. How all the alphabet
falls from my hands. I feel beneath my skin

the little needles of a life. I listen
whenever an intersection calls, I obey

its schizophrenia, an understanding of the art
in me that cries for me to act.

What I mean by hurt is that the hours,
they lie to me. I have been, but am not limited to,

a tense. Scars personify the mouth, too fragile
to sing or be. At the sills, estuaries. At the sorrows,

speech. I drink at the dream's atmospheric
embrace, I feed the mouth that bites me.

I become what is running through the woods.
Like armor unworn, I pose my battle

along the wall, plain as a god, singing like a verb,
sadistic. I wince and bleed with the world

and all its seamless ways to be rid of me,
until its complications octopus in my irises,

until the moment becomes my mother's sleeve
I once forgot to grasp.

Stockholm Syndrome with Death as the Captor

I have a feel I never say.
I have an honest weight.
I have one intense amen to whisper
in an attempt to keep heaven at the reins.

I lie nightly in a pewter state, wishing
I were free. Dying taunts me with its hiss
and haunt, so broad they are the whole
of me. The mouth of me is bitten off.

The cries of rooks form an abbey
in my heart. It is a havoc, wanting this.
A damage done, a hatched abyss, a witchcraft
of sobs where my quails hinge their nests.

The women of my lovelike wrists, who
arch their backs, white and skied with
lily skins. Riddles the world weaves even as
I watch. The same terrible dream I had

when the west wind came and the ages
said my name through the windows.
Infinity then, like a sever of stars.
Atmospheric, the gods gone wrong.

Memory sprinkled into the blood,
starstuck and with a honeycomb of rooms.
Its wounds pouring tongues tart as wine.
Its thousand hallucinations weep,

until the cities in the eyes are ruined hungers.
What the rain already knows. All its stoles
remember. Bayonets used to trim the symptoms
back. Close enough to the equator for

my instruments to lie, I have no nights but
the sighs I'd say and the seas I couldn't measure.
The sinews of the past are the source of this.
I pray to their gnarled exposure.

Phobia

I cannot choose. The world is too old.
On my knees before the first leaves to open.

I listen at the gaps in the floorboards
for someone who is listening for me,

but all I find is a death that looks like
the seed for something soft.

I remember rooms speaking back and forth.

I barely eat for fear of poison.
Species of homicide catch in my throat.

Into somewhere all the channels
are slipping, the near migration and the voice.

I only understand pain by what peels
from me when the heat is too much,

as if when the wind came for the pines
I called it good, I called it a form

of cathedral. I say no to a house
made mostly of eaves: no one

lives there. The wind lets no one in.

Hemorrhage

And the blood is a mad or a fast fast thing.
And the black sing of wind huge against the pane.
Small marrow of wind not wishing us well.

The herds because, by now, the miraculous
are beasts. The loss because we weep.
The long hair of a girl. The slow, divine decay.

Rows of infinite rain blossoming to sound,
gone to husk over the long summer's seed.
Rows of weeds cracked like bracken lips:

shepherds ending where the wolves begin.
It takes breath to say this kind of stink.
It takes all we remember to know what

we think. No one walks the land behind
the house. No one reads by the light
between cracks. No one is a passenger.

No one knows what such elegy means.
No one in the dancehall can remember
the name of the one they hold, no one

knows the wind has changed, no one knows
the priest has locked the door to the church
and the last of the whiskey was drunk last week.

Somnambulism

I dream enraged light in the eyes of cathedrals.
Objects like flesh infecting our mouths,

the curriculum of salt my body is,
toxic as the daughterless hills.

The corrugated waking found lately
in my voice is the one sob the dove made
that became the moon.

I dream what God calls the elements. Adrift,

with oars lowered to the task, the object of me
flown from the roost.

A hungry downriver in my voice.
Sleep has gray and vocal ruins.

I have a little god in me
and she doesn't cry at last.

Empathy

I wait for the pity to take effect.
It comes in a pill like a jewel
one only wears to church. It comes
like the fish killed to measure
the depth of the river. It comes
as a voice filled like a glass
with all the forgery such animals
can drink. They see themselves
in it. They mistake themselves
for gods, with the stars in the background
erased. They mistake themselves for
women who dance like half-moths
at the sill. Tense with it, I wait.
The pity begins to take effect.
The darknesses inside me shape,
like a village of soldiers asleep
in a horse. Armed to the teeth.
Armed with such faith.
The little flame begins in me.
I feel it like a bride. I feel it
like drops of blood in the snow.
My skin changes with the suffering
of others. My skin grows changed
with the process of awake.
I love the leap and the touch of day
as it hunts me from the window.
Summer takes effect. A crash
of poppies. The mowed fields like
a smother of elegies. I sip at

the photograph I make sitting
silent, crying someone else's pain,
my name forgotten, my mouth
a fat remember always saying what
it wants, nerve endings mapping all that's
offstage as reactions disaster my face.

Afterburn

Things too thin inhabit our dreams and we take on
their starving. We live until hunger

takes on such a shape that it is shoulder blades
in everything and sounds up in the trees. Then,

such ghosts. Such bones without skins doubled over.
A starless night every night and starlessness

is ashes or newsprint on the hands. Living
is barely a flock of birds the way it moves

like falling; it must be the cure for something,
the last lit house on a dead end street

or a hunger with two minds, drawing children
to the damp sheds at the far fence of their yards.

There is an entire August storm in everything said,
and to open the violent hives of remembering,

we imagine marigolds, birds drowned in the creek,
the lights left on in a room left behind.

The self is not a battery of tests.

Interview under Hypnosis

Describe what you would have seen had the roosters
woken you closer to dawn.

Late August already. The jagged at their sins.
God crouching at the labor of us, us crouching

at the labor of ourselves, with iron rods sewn
inside our clothes to keep our glass bodies

from breaking. Listening shivers at
the nerve endings. Things unfailingly cringe.

Describe being endangered.

I hear reasons not to cry but I am crying to feel
the cold come in like an illness that will recover me.

A bruise finds me, a bruise knows where I sleep:
the pear's sickly skin the color of a throat,

ravines that sing where ravines never were,
the sky in igneous ropes.

Describe being unreal.

When I finally woke, what was the world
but sleep. Graveyards where the wind is why,

wild as cursive and motorcycle-stark and white
as a gown of waiting. I am melting toward a world,

the small belly, into vivid such-liquids and
a disguise of lavishes. October lacerations.

The neon nears. No one tells me what
to believe and for once I believe in nothing.

Rorschach Test

The rooks flying out from a burning house
are in themselves the collapse of the eaves.

Their grief has the hands of any man's whisper,
the hiss of the falls being combed to sleep.

Winter is the heart eating out of the hand.
Its wail has a body of water.

Days scrape their hooves at the frozen ground:
past tenses crying in odd, pale shapes,

hours schizophrenic as weeds. Opposites mate
in the mouths of gods, animal-black, taloned,

asbestos-filled to blaspheme the sleepless blood.
All the wing structures filling endlessly.

The pupil is a human face filled with misery.
Its movement through the trees builds a blueprint

for uprooting, a roulette to be repeated
until the reams of memory run out.

Polygraph Test

I confess to the hemlock
in your drink. I confess to
the gods, to the gutter
intention. I confess
to the doorway creep.

Your kingdom of birds
that burn like vowels in relation
to the antidote you feign.

I cut from your lapels
the climate we create.

I confess the porcelain cup,
the evening smash, the portrait
of your moleculed complexities.
I confess to the no I have
placed in your heart.

I confess to the syringes
filled with bleach. I
confess to the memory,
the shoes, to the cold I
replenish in your name. I
fenced your waking in
with the old without,

the leaving, the inability
to breathe. I confess me
real. When the two
of us close in combat,
I will act the magician,
I will mimic the remedy.
I confess the minor earthquake
our velocity remains.

X-Ray of a Rib Cage

Doves multiply as if furious, as if fevered
by legible light. Absence of the heart.
Absence of the ambulance passing, quiet

in temper, strangled by night. The contrast
smears like coal in the stove of all these days,
bringing the horizon halfway to blackness,

taking away the self with no intention
of returning it. Each row makes a photograph
of ghosting, vertebrae the teeth in what must change.

When joy is hollow armor, fractures can be seen
where clean breaks are imagined; in a world
where nothing is clear, the world is a wound.

The Smoldering Hand

For all the things I realize, there are things
I won't admit. Never and always sleep so close
their hair intertwines and tangles as they twist.

I close my eyes to this as I open them
to the hospitals that admit me for short periods
of time. The nurses know I am going home, and so

I heal. Sometimes this means ignoring the nudity
of a quiet day. It means looking beyond
the transparency of passing cars, and sometimes

refusing to see romance as an omen,
until my most appropriate hours are spent
without sorrow, without its woven coat, with

my hands free for protection or gestures or love.
What is sorrow but emptiness and the sheer gasoline
that fills it? Its wind belongs in the wild mane

the way it does not belong in my throat.
Each time it escapes it leaves grief to linger
along the soft rim that gutters each sound.

I would close myself off if I could. I would
run the pasture until my legs lengthened
and became slender. But this weight I hold

like a bird in the hand and close to the chest
beats quickly and keeps me bold. Any moments
I steal have the short life span that comes

with flight. If I ask the nights to live longer,
they will whiten and retire. If I ask the tidal pools,
they will rise in temperature until the sea retrieves them.

If I ask the most natural afternoon, the one
I live according to, it will predict a winter
every year. It will predict no end to weather.

Sound of Eye, Wind, and Limb

My infants slept when their bodies needed sleep,
impostors in luxurious gowns. My infants felt unloved
by others while others loved the man-made things,
as though they were dolls in a house.

One night, I dreamed wind tunnels
containing many small wheels, I dreamed
one form with many faces saying,
the wire cutters are all in your mind.

My children being melted snow, I was
never afraid of their perpetual motion.
Sometimes the suffocation broke me.
Sometimes the breaking was good.

One night I woke to their gentle fingers raising
my eyelid with the lashes while they looked into
my eye, not daring to come near, not daring to keep
their distance while its forged identity watched.

Eye

An exotic patina, the reefs we stray onto, a deepening
of rooms. Your breathings stretch the nets of fishermen,
such groomed and tangled manes. The surface of your lake

is torn paper, the rain-soaked hides of horses.
You discover what the sea represents in dreams
and are discovered by the subtle nocturne in mourning.

Without your garden, the statue's reach is armless,
has a snow that has ashes that can amputate our calm.
In you, a woman sews beside her sleeping child,

the man with the hunched back weeps. What little light
there is strains through night's black and central pierce;
what grief, what rows of houses because we live.

The self is not what is said about the self.

Autobiography toward a Study
of the Thousand Wounds

Doctor, this is my diary. It begins with my confession to you.

I was hung before my throat could cry the rivers. I was hung
like an animal and the rope had a bite: when I touch, I touch
a razor of teeth, an amen on the edge of each of them. I am
adrift. I can see the pier with the loose rope fallen. I can see
the fog and the oars that will not last. I have eyes that are lan-
terns so I will not wreck. And yet I cannot steer myself toward
land. I am at the end of risk. I am at the end of my fragment-
ing hands. I only have nerves to tell me how far. I only have
nerves; the rest of me is ill. What I twist into rears toward
frost. I twist into the immigrant rain. I am again at sea, made
sick with floating. As it is, I am rich with different versions of
myself, and I do not know an antidote for me.

I am an impossible equation proven to exist. With the ache of
layers yet to peel off, made of features and a clockwork heart
whose mechanism breaks as death sits, wreckage in the face,
smells foul, and is blackened. Accidental fracture is a gift.

What I see is not so much a lost figure as an arch of rain, so
many windows, and an expression like wool. What I see is not
so much the fields of me as the silver beneath, the skeleton,
its trace elements, as one falls to the hands and knees. What
I see is not so much the childhood collapse or the stories the
sea-branches cherish and break, or the way I move air in front
of me from its delicate weave. What I see is a child's breath at

the shoulder like a thief. A chemistry of sin that earns our keep.
That makes of me an enemy when the enemy is scarce.

I cannot remember my guilt, my personal plague is one of
indifference: my house is built of ill dreams, a desire to do harm,
the sick art of the act. The struggle is a thing I scrape free:
random cloaks or shadows across my lips that keep what I say
as the oath I have sworn. What I would have said terrifies the
masses. What I would have said threatens with the large hand,
with planets askew, with what I knew was wrong from the
moment I thought it.

Doctor, there are too many nests for me. To list. To sit and see.
To frequent. To invent. I count them out, sticks and rakes, ribs
and rags, a fathom I can wreck. To sense. To taste. These are
the prophecies where the whisperings can live. I sift them and
wait. I shake them and end. I am the land. By the flesh of the
world, I crush and flee. I seize and cry. I am the mind of me. I
singe and crave. The nothing of me crude. I am soothed from
it.

Autobiography with God Complex and Epidemic

I have always been a statue, my absence
of gestures just right, my eyes too clean,
my knees oiled, all parts of me draped.

The corridors of me whisper with chains. I try
to make a language from the splendid voids of rain.
I try to be nourished by what has been inedible.

Then I starve. I am shocked by the begging bowls
present in my hands. I pass through ghosts
of my own gone self. The little winds

that are its pulse. The little innards that
keep it hot. The jolt of it is near enough.
The art of it is tapered shut.

My image thins and cracks like the high notes
of a choir. The most outward parts of me
fix and flex. Neat sutures border this:

a kiss of whim, a stitch of thistle, a lick
of phobias. A fidget of shivers winds its way
in. My mind is a lamplight for silence.

My heart fashioned of artificial ash, my heart
a divan of shadows. That geography of palpitations,
my heart: it houses thousands of embers.

What is shark-like. What is frayed. Its requiems
lend luminosity. Bewitched interiors,
pale and collective. A blue significance of trees.

I fast while others feast. My soul: its electrical
quarries. I am sated by my brought mouths.
I am quiet by their lakes. The eye in me

drowns. The brow in me bleeds. I can seem
dim. I am at rest. As the ghosts that rule flesh
die in its bed, their syntax scaffolding the breath.

Autobiography in Not-Song and October

How the locusts came. As though the rain
were not enough. As though its blood
were never shed. As though its animals
needed shelter. How the truth came,
a trick. A shift or northern exposure.

How the sleep came, a downdraft
of birds. Then lay newborn
and steady in a bloodstream of light.
Its river had a slip of bodices.
I was its faithful wife. I was
the knife of its fishlike satin,
the roads it bares like teeth.

I was the one need it had,
for darkness. I laughed my darkness
to the trees; its wind made
sewing needles of the grasses.
The river or city's guitar-hard weep.

Soon after, snow fell between the rows
of corn and the brittle uncut stalks
trembled, mottled as the scales of fish.
The world drowsed. The birds knew.
So flesh and bone. So old. So blessed.

The little moon of my arrival
set, my bent hand singing, a sound,
a threat, my being a braid

of aching and text. My selves
traveled death, bare in its garment.

My next wound was a form of waking,
the wound that hadn't happened yet.
The night had sails like the eyes
of us starving. The wind speaking loss
for us, the shallow balance singing.
Each second on the clock was a harbor,
but my ships, they would not rest.

What the Cultivation Means

I have been good. I am not allowed to dream.
Each of the seasons I am not allowed to touch.

Long long grass. The long impossible strings
of pearls I once believed were days. Little boys

singing a fabric of lambs. The one blue iris
to remind me of earth, the feast of hours

riding sidesaddle through the streets. Slightly
acidic and sleepless in the wild. So so sad.

How will I eat? The silos are empty. I am
not allowed to sleep or monitor my wounds.

The Unspeakable, Said

When the sky inside me is the same as the sky,
an afternoon has fallen loose from the bells.

Its water sheds to a field mute with poppies.
Its waves are dark horses' heads lowering, thrown.

Daily, I hear instinct turn back at the undergrowth;
daily, the night is a city of spires,

a scrap of cloth cutting scenes within scenes.
How to stand among its branches and not feel broken.

The flights of birds unlace the sky, and still
some fashion scissors and sever to sleep.

When the wind calls what comes wild-eyed to answer,
birds cry a child making newspaper dolls.

The highway is the longing in all of us.
The white edge of death begins burning down:

my word a small word on a small white page.
My wrist's opal river has spilled from the sleeve.

Conjugating the Void

And I was as cold as the cold root goes,
sources of calling and folded of shade,
knotted of weed and a loosening parting,
I was as cold as the sank ghost does.

And I was as real as the blue unraw,
as naked as amen, as awkward as old,
round as a grieving and ancient unfasten,
I was as real as the ill scrawl of love.

And I was as near as the first moon rounded,
as god-like as sinking and making of light,
as mired by law as the ignorant thousand,
as grave as the pages revisioned in time.

And I was as lost as the famine of living,
as cordless and horrid and envied and dead.
All of the my was a reason to take me:
I believed the lies the world made flesh.

The self is not a study of the world.

There Remain New Branches

I can imagine such a place: like a flute, it comes apart.
Streets loosen like tobacco. There are animal skins.

It comes across, the way bodies' crying reaches us
and crawls inside. It is beyond the mirrored room

of my sister's eye. It has such a dark iris no light
comes through, and the shed light of rain becomes

a neutral sound. Here, we remember what it's like
to remember. Naming parts of the body, we find

they are familiar. Dreams never make the transfer
to days, and the gladioli are wilting.

Welcome to changing everything. Welcome to starving
out of sleep. By morning, weariness will have replaced

the jawbone of a thinned and willful sky.
This illness is savage. These clouds, they are scythes.

World Hypothesis

The geese again.
Each call is a rent
in the rouse it have
felt. Each soiled thing
ratchets it back until
it bland with the hinge
or begin to hear,
clairvoyant. Now the absent
martyr, it go netted when
it go, and guilt is its
inhibitor. Words lamb
like little kings, killed
for their thrones. It feel
then the drop calculate
in it, it feel the shadow
level for flight. The geese
frond, models to the eye,
missing the world by
a margin. The sky wipes
itself clean, it feel genes
in it calculate, a hammer
fall, it feel itself
treading water.

The Zoology of Imaginary Joy

Then nightfall came while I was still
knitting it, hollowed with air and the velvet
of throats, riddled with grit and mossless

lengths, riddled with the remains of animals.
Carried toward this, by wind or by waking
among the reeds on a day it is raining,

a dustless fall of light. What is there
to bloom for here, what is there to do but pray
and save the emptiness for later, those lairs

toward October, no rinds, no sweet or seedless flesh.
The years fall open like petals or flocks, forked
or episodic, coffins of the wilderness to open

and become, sieve through which my roots seek
the sleeping lambs of answers, those fallow fields,
those clicking strokes of oars in place.

I would find the corridor and walk it to its end
where there is sure to be a window looking out
on the tidy yards of those who are craving.

This is the charred behavior. This is witnessing
within slow motion the going wheel of dreams
as its barns lean or buildings burn to the ground.

The Botany of Man-Made Things

They groomed the long throats of seabirds.
Stars schooled inside every barrel and spackled

the clearings there. Dogs scratched at back doors.
There were things winded, white, swordlike and edible.

Most unnatural was the applause of leaves:
it lacked the crackle of an umber wing.

But nothing is such a sword, running the sun
from its tip. Not even forests. Not even fields.

The garden was corrupted by pumpkins; some of the wounds
wouldn't close. New places came, places that flies,

upon seeing, divide out as scenes. They watched
what they thought was ownership burn toward

the world, along a road broken off at the stem
and into gullies scraping like shins at the dam.

Memory:

long in my veins like a country
of water, long like whispers darker
than the bronze of plums, than
the silence prized from the layman's
mouth. No counting down
to the catastrophe here.
No autumn mix of laughter.

If I were awake, the gallows
inside me would trouble
and take, lay of the land,
anger or sun. I have never
remembered the tightening
of ropes. I have never
remembered the reason.

Theory of Relativity

The diameter of a bicep is the diameter of my heart.
The pigeons are the river, the river is rain.

The anorexia of branches is not to be compared.
July beading sweat when the screen door slams,

my glance the smaller animal and the stark beyond
of snow. For once, the mind slows.

And when the streets turn back from the night
they pave, I am left on their dark stoop.

Paper cranes become guests of their pale bodies.
There is no sense answering such gray light.

Body Thesaurus

In your dream, the act of breathing is a red-headed girl
with a body lactose-pale and livid against the skin
of water. A crack along the porcelain cup of this,
colored all absinthe with you. The closed white shutters

of your backbone as you sleep toward wrists spilling
their listless snowflakes farther south. Mouth:
night's lilacs branching insolubly. Hair hissing, stems.
Mouth: the hospital: your houses are asking chemicals

out of the dark. Your lids are the lime-lined,
impromptu graves of thieves. As a mind,
your body is a wall of leaves; let its edges whisper
a collage of liquids singing, lips, the sangria weeds.

The self is not a cure.

Antidote with Attempts at Diagnosis

They did the test of the body placed beside a flint-skinned nurse,
the test for epidemics formed of mirrors, the test of the lethal pills
hidden in the eyeglasses.

They did the flow of sodium ions into nerve cells, they did filth
in each of the orifices, they did a gem, a pollen shape, they did a
transfusion to the vein.

They kept evolving unpredictable results, found a vertigo of snakes
and called it the mind, found time and called us its puppets.

They began to sense eternity and accumulate remorse.

They filmed the corrosion each touch would cause, test for
hemorrhaging, test for poison, test for the memory of adolescent faith.

They found the secret room where all the genomes drape. They
closed a hand's palm made of images over all nomadic sleep.

They found a landscape in the eye, doing its quiet singing.

They mixed situations to administer with the full complexity of
weather, mixed the plumage of unmade bones with their gutterless
fray, with a thaw as raw as speech, to help them fracture like timbers
or a dove's cluttered voice.

They proceeded with medications, experimental embalming, anorexic
restoration, therapeutic disturb.

They admitted an inability.

They lost count of the dying. They fished infants from the creek.

They slept in proximity of the mouths of others to be somewhat like breath.

Antidote with Placebo

Pit yourself against gutted ships, against
the lips of those you love the least, against
the hollows where quails spend their lives.

Do not sleep. Do not take shape.
Ambush the soft armies of seas and the singular
face of an adjacent cliff. Scream the way

everything screams. Find a small longitude
to stitch along the coast. Find an iodine
to dye your dreams. Find a decade. Deny

your face. Deny the very steps you take,
three times before the cock crows.
Never pace. Never betray your need.

Never drink the nocturne's blood.
Become a lion who obeys the whip, become
a tiger in a cage. Become the rage that never fits,

the metal, the release. Challenge yourself against
the streets. Cradle your head in your hands.
Be chaste. Drop a kerchief from a windowed

train. See yourself as a curb blurred by water,
stagnant, layered in grease. Grow untender.
Grow corrupt. Strangle your reason to within

an inch of its life. Focus like a machine.
Then find the city, the stink of steam.
The soft demeaning face of light

the traffic will give off. Grab the distance
from your heart and rust with it in
your hand. Understand the starve

and feast. Understand the stop and start.
The slaughter. The plea for release.
Drop the suit of your self with its solitary pelt

and debris of autumn leaves, with its chrome
to row through and feel alive, with its miles
as herons on a lake. Soon you will wake,

so doctor your corpse. Let the scissors
scathe you to lyres. Operate while it's still day.
Then drop the body onto its clockwork of joints,

onto its lace of nerves, onto the curves
of its spine and its place. Check for breath
at the entrance of its arch. Check for breath

at the gangway of its waist. Let it drop
once you have worshipped the nurture,
the circle of thorns it remains.

Antidote with Beatitudes

Blessed are the indifferent, for they shall never weep.
Blessed are the bewildered, for they shall soon forgive.
Blessed are those who beg for sadness until their marrow breaks.
Blessed are those who let gone be gone.
        What hooks you breaks you. Rides you clean.
Blessed are those who have no self to say amen to,
        to trawl for them while they sleep.
Blessed are those who define the world as some slipped thing,
        some bitter tantrum. They shall know the world.
Blessed are those who, with a foreign tongue,
        speak asters as the language of the rain.
Blessed are those for whom sin is a saint.
        They shall go down on their knees,
        the sails of their pale faces turned from any wind.
Blessed are those whose chalices are filled with an arid semantics.
        They shall vomit at night every perfection of the body.
Blessed are those for whom the sound of memory has a sharpness
of violins.
        They shall feel scaffolding deep in the blood.
Blessed are those who walk a shoreline while its whispers swarm.
        Meaning is a bird call in the interim.

Antidote with Early Weather

My white autumn. Its letters to me.
It sings France in the shadow of the moon
and I listen. It calls me morning.
It burns over and over with the wish to be
new. It ferns like lightning over the skin,
small invisible. It ends, in awe
of the corset's threshold since this
love affair began. Whatever rib bones
it had were replaced with water. Whatever
hour it had was a ruby in my brooch.
Small wind through loose hands, branching
where the oceans meet, small wind
through ripped fabric as villages
give off doves of breath. Anthills
dream, the ivy drifts, axes cleave
the crusting wood. My white autumn
lies in the mouths of the fed, on the lapels
of children, a treason of gulls
hungry for gladness, and sad as the sea.

Antidote with Symptoms

The backdrop for us is the pandemic awake.
Melancholy as the cut of rubies. An older
siege. Our eyelids of silk are speech.

The backdrop for us is a kettle of vultures;
our pupils form a climate the genuine call
elegy. We know it is a moment or abyss.

We map its madameless countries.
Secrets shed unceremonious as swans
and tell our hands which hands to hold;

the backdrop for us is a little seep of slowly.
No one looks. No one contaminates this
dead voltage that falls between the stars.

Black is the color of our unspilled blood; its hooves,
unshod in winter, approach from the direction
of the world. Voices rise, bizarre miles in them.

We are lost at taut as it eyes the throat,
its heart's chaste orphanages and mimicry
of birds, its barbers responsible for bloodletting.

Tourniquet

It was a small wound but it was my wound,
and a ceremony happened between us.

It was a small love I felt pantomime near my mouth,
those moths with the solitude of sulfur for wings.

It was a small return, half-spoken,
yet pure enough to maintain.

Sharp: it burned twice as long at the sight of loss.
It burned like a woman with her arms stretched toward the sea.

It learned the shape of my blood like malaria.
It mothered the shape of my twisted belief.

It may have felt what I felt for a time: the entire
world beginning its carnivorous unlatching.

It may have appeared less frequently, less
fragile, been a wince or what coincidence cringing.

And still its moon like a blind eye's twin.
Each sound's overcoat caught in the trees.

It was not my dream, it was not my reason,
tensing like bowstrings with the arrows of pain.

It was more like the ashes I found in the mirror
when I went there to look at my face.

Preventing a Relapse

If you begin with the moths,
their bodies marred to a dark vernacular,
their stars more savage than the excellent seas,

their sob of crows with coal-born wings,
their scansions of the lullaby rain,
their boneless worship longer than the wind.

If your luck runs out when the tide comes in.
If you pry the barb from the appetite beast.
If you hang the sky from its collapsed-rag wings,

their antithesis of candelabras.
If you sleep on a plain reed mat. Are glad
for dusk that dances silence half to death,

one minute ordinary, delinquent the next.
If you let each moment fragment like the moon.
Linger with the sky the pigeons ask

while going down to their now-dry rivers.
If you let your skin feel the relent.
If you elegize the soft occasion.

Wholeness Is an Imagined State

Or myth: a giver of consolation prizes,
hands bitten black and blue, gods
we knew who had no wings: it's not
the blood's sigh. It is the cry of the unborn,

held back in half-formed throats, in
the vocal chords of those who know death
before they know a prose where the mouth
of it is hunger, the mouth of it is heat,

a beat of cells where the skies go blank
with their frail gowns. Machines that sound
the argue of awake, rust and decay as
there bloats a foundry of rhythms or hymns.

The wish seems to unravel. An aphrodisiac
too often on the plate, a skin or seed
tough while the teeth shut and shudder
and, like a lit kettle, shiver and shake.

It is not the blood, it is not the face, it is
the greed, it is the mute need of the broken
clock gasping its oar-handed rasping to three.
We hear the root's sure grave tapping to drink

from the runoff, the suburbs, the factory,
the ceiling fan blades, their slow, weighted
circumferences as it fills our china plates.
We sit and eat, and spend the day.

It is not the vein, this fever pitch, this
million states of evil. It is not the trait
of an inherited gene, it is not inherited:
it is ours to take. What being means

is a trick that brightens. One finds oneself
queen among the dead. One finds oneself draped
in ashes and made. The shapes of rain and
candid lenses. The facts of hammer and grease.

Acknowledgments

Grateful acknowledgment is made to the editors of the following journals, in which these poems first appeared:

32 Poems: "Phobia" and "Rorschach Test"

American Letters & Commentary: "Antidote with Beatitudes"

Anti-: "Autobiography with Not-Song and October," "Stockholm Syndrome with Death as the Captor," and "Wholeness Is an Imagined State"

Boston Review: "Interview under Hypnosis"

Green Mountains Review: "Personality State: Animal," "Personality State: Husk," and "Personality State: Statue"

Greensboro Review: "Somnambulism"

Gulf Coast: "Eye" and "Felon's Logic"

Indiana Review: "Antidote with Attempts at Diagnosis" and "Antidote with Symptoms"

The Kenyon Review: "Personality State: Prophet" and "Personality State: Scavenger's Daughter"

The Laurel Review: "Body Thesaurus" and "Polygraph Test"

Midway Journal: "Personality State: Persephone"

New Orleans Review: "Conjugating the Void," "Preventing a Relapse," "Sound of Eye, Wind, and Limb" and "The Zoology of Imaginary Joy"

The North American Review: "The Skins We Slit Seeking the Vertebrae of Snakes"

Ploughshares: "Antidote with Placebo"

Prairie Schooner: "The Botany of Man-Made Things"

Quarterly West: "Memory:" (as "Definition of Recollection"), "The Unspeakable, Said," "What the Cultivation Means" and "World Hypothesis"

So and So Magazine: "Empathy" and "Hemorrhage"

Verse: "Afterburn," "There Remain New Branches" and "X-Ray of a Rib Cage"

Women's Studies Quarterly: "Autobiography with God Complex and Epidemic"

"Autobiography with God Complex and Epidemic" was awarded honorable mention in the *Gulf Coast* Poetry Contest.

"Personality State: Prophet" was chosen by Mark Strand for inclusion in *Best New Poets 2008.*

"Phobia" appears in *Old Flame: From the First 10 Years of* 32 Poems Magazine, edited by Deborah Ager, Bill Beverly and John Poch.

"The Smoldering Hand" first appeared in *The Anthology of New England Writers,* edited by Frank Anthony and Susan Anthony.

"There Remain New Branches" appears in *Verse: The Second Decade,* edited by Brian Henry.

The poem "World Hypothesis" was featured on the *Verse Daily* web site.

Thank you to the New Hampshire State Council on the Arts and to I-Park Artists' Enclave for the gifts of time and space, which made possible the writing of these poems, and to Cynthia Huntington, Cate Marvin, Lauren Raine, and G. C. Waldrep for support and inspiration. I am also continually grateful for the miraculous work of everyone at Tupelo Press. Thank you, Jeffrey Levine and Jim Schley, Rose Carlson and Marie Gauthier, for all you do.

Other Books from Tupelo Press

See our complete backlist at www.tupelopress.org

CPSIA information can be obtained at www.ICGtesting.com
Printed in the USA
BVOW080108040413

317238BV00001B/3/P